This journal belongs to

Date

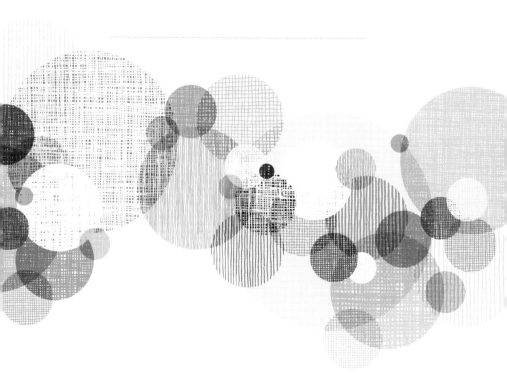

$\mathcal{W}$e have only this moment,
sparkling like a star in our hand—
and melting like a snowflake.

FRANCIS BACON

Wherever you are,
be all there.
JIM ELLIOT

Much of what is sacred is hidden in the ordinary, everyday moments
of our lives. To see something of the sacred in those moments takes
slowing down so we can live our lives more reflectively.

KEN GIRE

Be.
Here.
Now.

To lie sometimes on the grass under the trees on a summer's day, listening to the murmur of water...is by no means a waste of time.
SIR JOHN LUBBOCK

A mindful person relishes wisdom.

THE BIBLE

Sometimes all you need is a new perspective.
Try changing your viewpoint.

Start where you are.
Use what you have.
Do what you can.
ARTHUR ASHE

What you get by achieving your goals is not as important as what you become by achieving your goals.
ZIG ZIGLAR

The secret of the future is hidden in our daily routines.

The reason people awaken is because they have finally stopped agreeing to things that numb their souls.

Learn to be what you are, and learn to resign with good grace all that you are not.
HENRI-FRÉDÉRIC AMIEL

An intentional life embraces only the things that will add
to the mission of significance.

*H*old close to your
essential self.

SHAUNA NIEQUIST

The slower the living, the greater
the sense of fullness and satisfaction.
ANN VOSKAMP

Sometimes the answer is to breathe and thank God for this very moment.

*D*on't hurry, don't worry. You're only here for a short visit so be sure to smell the flowers along the way.

WALTER HAGEN

You own the key
to your own
peace of mind.

Always be on the lookout for the presence of wonder.
E. B. WHITE

*A quiet mind
is able to hear
intuition
over fear.*

_____

_____

_____

_____

_____

_____

_____

_____

_____

_____

_____

_____

_____

_____

_____

_____

_____

_____

_____

The best thing you can do right now is to finish what you started
last year and not let those good intentions grow stale.

THE BIBLE

Mindfulness is being present without judgment in every single moment.

Take time to notice all the usually unnoticed, simple things in life.
Delight in the never-ending hope that's available every day!
GLADYS TABER

The most precious gift you can offer anyone is your attention.

Being mindful simply means being aware of everything
about this moment and giving your full attention to it.

*T*alk to yourself
like you would
to someone
you love.
BRENÉ BROWN

The greatest weapon against stress is our ability
to choose one thought over another.
WILLIAM JAMES

Ellie Claire
Hachette Book Group
1290 Avenue of the Americas, New York, NY 10104
ellieclaire.com

First Edition: June 2019

Ellie Claire is a division of Hachette Book Group, Inc. The Ellie Claire name and logo are
trademarks of Hachette Book Group, Inc.

The publisher is not responsible for websites (or their content) that are not owned by the
publisher.

Scripture taken from The Message. Copyright © 1993, 1994, 1995, 1996, 2000, 2001, 2002.
Used by permission of NavPress Publishing Group. All rights reserved.

Print book interior design by Bart Dawson.

ISBN 978-1-63326-214-0 (softcover)

Printed in China

RRD-S

10   9   8   7   6   5   4   3   2   1